JOURNEY OF LIGHT

PAMELA J. OLYNEK

WESTBOW
PRESS®
A DIVISION OF THOMAS NELSON
& ZONDERVAN

WestBow Press books may be ordered through booksellers or by contacting:

WestBow Press
A Division of Thomas Nelson & Zondervan
1663 Liberty Drive
Bloomington, IN 47403
www.westbowpress.com
1 (866) 928-1240

ISBN: 978-1-5127-4304-3 (sc)
ISBN: 978-1-5127-4305-0 (e)

Print information available on the last page.

WestBow Press rev. date: 5/27/2016

DEDICATION

To my spiritual sister Darlene, whose walk with God inspires me, whose laughter fills me with joy and whose friendship is a gift I hold in my heart.

PREFACE

I have decided to write a second book. Once again, I feel inspired from within to do this. The title <u>Journey of Light</u> comes to my mind and feels right. Gradually, over time, this seed of a second book begins to sprout. It comes to me that I will share meaningful glimpses of my own life. Ideas of a format come to mind and soon I am accumulating pages of scrawled notes.

My hope is the reader will recall incidents within their own life journey, incidents of Divine synchronicities and grateful blessings.

Our life is indeed a product of our choices. Yet, I believe as well, we are often guided to those choices. At times in my life, it feels like God has set out bumper cars on my path, keeping me going in a specific direction, one that is always for my highest good. Perhaps, as you read these entries from my life journey, you will come to recognize God's hand in your own life.

For those who have yet to develop this personal relationship with the Divine, may these pages hold inspiration and a calling for you to reach out to Him in prayer. He is there.

This journey is not a merry go round. So please do not assume you know the book by glancing at the first few pages. Such a journey is ever changing, ever evolving, taking one in new directions. That is part of its beauty, its elegance.

INTRODUCTION

There may be times in your life when you feel lost and confused. Do not despair. Welcome these troublesome feelings for they can be motivators for change and growth.

My own life is at times filled with such confusion over which path to take. Yet these times continually propel me forward on my 'Journey of Light.' I am able to even be grateful for these periods in my life for now I bow my head in prayer knowing I am never alone.

It is important to not reach out for drugs, alcohol, meaningless sex, another relationship, fancier toys, more work, and/or less play. None of these actions will bring you the truth your soul is seeking. Better to look within for the answers and guidance. I invite you now to join me as I share from my journals excerpts of my own journey.

1

I am flying out to Vancouver to participate in Werner Erhard's EST Training. Werner Erhard is the founder of the EST training. (It began in 1971 and dissolved in 1984.) EST is the Latin word for 'to be.' His workshops are opening up a whole new way of approaching life. It is becoming popular quickly. Werner uses music and lyrics throughout his seminars. Messages come through in song, matching what he is illustrating in his workshops. He talks about the quality of our life being determined by the quality of our thinking, that our thoughts produce actions and our attitude is something over which we have control. His workshops and my participation in them alter the course of my life. Within a short time, I leave my failing marriage. I move to a new city with my two sons. I receive financial support while I go back to college. I am on my way to a brand new life.

However, before the end of the first year of

college in the Social Work Program, I hit bottom emotionally. I end up in a group therapy program at a hospital. It is explained to me that as I participated in the first year of my college studies, it stirred up my past, like a huge brewing pot. In the first year of the Program, the focus is on us, to be an effective worker; you need to have healed any past issues.

This results in years of intermittent counselling, most of which is one on one. I need to go back and heal the blocked childhood traumas before I am ever able to have a successful life. This begins my conscious 'Journey of Light.' I continue to do the necessary work to heal my life. It is only by going within and opening these closed doors of the past that I can have freedom in the present. This means freedom from the side effects of unhealed issues, like addictions and unhealthy relationships. It takes a lot of courage to open these doors. This journey brings one eventual freedom to embrace ones life fully.

Thank you Father for this 'Journey of Light.'

2

This is a time in my life when I need to step up to the plate and hit my own home run, not cheer on someone else.

Initially, this is my intention – to cheer on someone else as they go for help for their addiction issues. When they do not comply, I choose to look into the mirror and take an honest look at who is staring back at me.

On a leave from work, I have plenty of time to focus on getting strong and healthy. I establish an exercise room in the house and am on my way to becoming more physically fit. It is other areas of my life that need attention and for these I am seeing a counsellor.

Looking back at myself from the mirror, I make the decision to go to an AADAC Center for alcohol abuse. It is a live-in facility. The program lasts a few weeks.

During this time, I was out for a walk near the

treatment center. I enter a church. I sit on the steps to the altar and I pour out my heart to Jesus. Weeks later, I discover a picture of Jesus talking to His Father. Every time I look at this picture, I am reminded of that day.

As I write this, I gaze at that framed picture on my wall. The sun this morning is shining on it, creating a Heavenly glow.

Thank you Father for walking with me through that stormy time and still being there when the sun shone again in my life. Thank you so very much.

Amen.

3

I had to work through a lot of childhood issues with my father. I finally arrived at a place of forgiveness. I will share a letter I wrote.

'Dad, I want to take this opportunity to thank you for being the father you were over the years. Even though, I missed sharing a special closeness with you, there are many great, wonderful and honorable things you did, like the way you treated mom with honor, respect and love. I am glad I grew up in a home where that existed.

I am very grateful to you Dad for being such an excellent provider for our family. I never went hungry or without clothes. I always had a wonderful home. I was able to take dance classes, skating, swimming, baton and go to Brownies. We had wonderful summer holidays and great Christmases and birthday parties, all those fun experiences that many children never have. Thank you!

Mom and you provided stability in my life. I never had to worry about having a place to come home to or parents who loved me. I have so much to be grateful for.

Even though you found it difficult to show your children your love (due to your own upbringing,) you never let us down in other ways. You were not an alcoholic. You never hit me, you never lied to me, and you kept your word. You were faithful to my mother. You were a man of integrity. I remember our talks and your words of wisdom. I have drawn on those many times in my life. Thank you!

So Dad, I wanted you to hear all this and to remember it always. For even though our visits and talks on the phone may have been quiet and strained at times, underneath it all are these truths.

Being a parent myself now, all the mistakes I have made, I do realize one thing, that is that we each do our best at the time, with the wisdom and knowledge we have.

So Dad, as you enjoy the winter stage of your life, just remember you were a good dad, despite it all and that I do love you.

Speaking from my heart to yours,
Your daughter,
Pamela'

4

Our journeys through life, of course, include relationships. As an adult, it seems I am always
in a romantic relationship. It is a few months before
my fifty-third birthday. I feel I am finally ready to
be on my own.

In my relationships, as in my addictions, I am
unconsciously trying to fill a void. What I need is
right inside me, in my heart, where God placed it.
In time, my journey will lead me there.

Meanwhile, I waver. I re-enter a relationship that
is not in my best interest. Eventually, I am strong
enough to leave.

Each step of this journey is important. A friend,
wanting to make this clearer to me explained how
our relationships are like ingredients in a recipe. The
final product – ourselves – requires those ingredients
for us to become who we are today.

I am learning not to dwell in regret, shame or
guilt. I continue to learn that forgiveness is essential

on this 'Journey of Light,' forgiveness of self and others.

Now truly on my own, I am able to begin the important journey of self-love. This I am learning is a vital ingredient to a happy and peaceful life.

Thank you Father for this new understanding.

5

I am taking a class in the evening at a church near where I live. Taking a church class is something new for me. It is based on Max Lucado's book <u>Fearless</u> (Lucado, 2009.) A group of woman surround a table in a small room in the church building. There are several evenings to this class.

On the last night, something occurs that is forever imprinted on my mind, heart and soul. This 'something' changes my life forever more.

We are concluding the final night of the series. I have been participating fully all along which surprises me, for I am normally rather quiet and withdrawn. The leader suggests we end in prayer. My inner voice nudges me and I speak up, suggesting we stand up and hold hands for the closing prayer. We decide to move out into the larger open room beside us.

The circle forms, we bow our heads in prayer. The leader explains that others can follow her prayer aloud should they be inclined to do so. I look at my feet, aware that I am a part of this circle. Into my head pops a Bible verse: 'When two or three are gathered in my name there am I in the midst of them,' (KJV Matthew 18:20.) I close my eyes. I see chains around my ankles. Next, I see and feel these chains being broken. Instantly, I feel my life change. I am transformed. I open my eyes, my head still lowered in prayer. My tears splash onto the floor leaving little water puddles at my feet. I lift my head ever so slightly and see the woman across from me crying as well.

I am so grateful I spoke up and suggested we stand together, hands joined, empowering our connection to God.

Thank you Father for this amazing and memorable day!

6

Today I am being baptized. I am going up to the front to share before the actual ceremony. I raise my voice and speak.

"Since I made the decision a few weeks ago to be baptized today, I have gone through a range of emotions. I realize as soon as a person makes this choice, a process begins to unfold.

I have written out a few times now what I am going to say today. I knew I wanted to talk to God before my baptism so I knew my testimony would be in the form of a prayer. Finally, yesterday morning I wrote what I will read today. It took hours writing it out, crying, stopping, rereading it, and crying some more. This actually in itself had a cleansing effect. It also provided an opportunity to share some very special time with God.

Please bow your heads now and join me in prayer."

"Dear God in Heaven, when I awoke today I felt you ask me to think about the miracles in my life. You said to go over my life like a movie then to write about what I see.

I hear myself singing the song, 'Jesus loves me' over and over again for what seems like hours in my bedroom as a young girl. It gives me solace in a world where I feel afraid, alone and confused.

Next, I see myself attending church after my separation from my husband. Once again, I find comfort and protection. Protection from what I wonder, my own demise? Because of you, I am able to continue to love myself and my life, versus self-blame and self-destruction.

You saved us Father, all of us, when we were involved in a head-on collision. I can still clearly see my daughter's dad picking up her baby Jesus book off the highway. He looked at me and said, 'This is what saved us.'

God, you have been keeping an eye on me my whole life, even when I was not looking at you anymore. So many times I foolishly put myself in vulnerable situations where darkness could have prevailed. Instead you would send me an earth angel and keep me safe. Like the time I overdrank at the bar. I was headed for my car when a kind, sober person showed up and took care of me.

You have given me hope in times of despair. You have taught me to let go of the past, to release it. You have shown me that guilt and shame accomplish nothing. It is what I do now that matters.

At times, I will still see a scene from my past where I could have been a better mother. If I could do things again, I would change some choices I made back then. You gently and lovingly turn my head to the present and remind me that I am different now and that is what really matters. I still cry, when I think about that stuff. To know that something you have done or not done, has hurt your child, is a terrible thing.

God, you have taught me that it is who I am now that matters. It is through my commitment to my own wellness, to years of healing, that has brought me to this place today.

I feel I can be a beacon of Light for my children now. This is important to me. Dear God, you hear my daily prayer, that you will guide me, motivate me and direct me in any way I can assist my children on their journey.

Next, I recall when I could feel you lift me up and pull me out of a marriage that was sucking the life right out of me. You handled all the details and plopped me down in an apartment, with a job and in a place I had always dreamed of being. That indeed was a miracle.

Even when I wander off the path, you are still here with open arms when I finally find my way back.

I cried today when it hit me that the greatest miracle of all is your forgiveness and your total and unconditional love for all of us.

I have prayed so many times that you would take me and mould me like clay. More importantly, I have prayed that you would find me worthy to do so.

Now, as I write this this morning, I realize you already have done that molding. You have answered this prayer. You have taken me from a lost, confused, totally detached and unaware soul. I was one who lied, cheated and had addictions. I was one who was filled with darkness and despair. I was one who made unhealthy and selfish choices. You have brought me through this healing process one step at a time with your love and your guidance. You have filled me with such courage and faith, this shy timid scared little girl.

You have saved my life Father; the shallow and empty aspects of my life are gone. Instead there is a peace, a strength, a faith and a love that no person or any situation can shatter. That in itself is a miracle.

Now, as I walk my daily path with you, my needs are always met. I have only to keep my eyes on you and keep my faith.

I now stand humbly before you Father, feeling so grateful and so blessed.

This is such an honour today, to be baptized in your name. As I step into this water today, I declare to the world you are my one and only God. I declare that Jesus is indeed my Savior. By his name, all my sins are washed away and my relationship with you Father will last forevermore.

I love you Heavenly Father, with all my heart and soul.

Amen."

7

It is Saturday. I am at a women's spiritual retreat. I am so grateful to be here. I am sitting by a lake, the sun is warm on my skin, the wind blows gentle.

I received a gift earlier this morning. In my heart and mind I felt Jesus presence so clearly, much clearer than ever before. I felt Him, so real so loving, so peaceful.

Donna, our speaker, is talking about God being in control, allowing and surrendering as we accept that versus us wanting to always be in control. I recall this past week with my son moving back to BC and how hard this is. I hear my inner voice telling me over and over, 'God loves you Pam. God loves you.' I am being reassured that I am not alone during this change. This morning at the retreat I hear this message with new ears.

Donna is showing us a print of Jesus holding a baby lamb (KJV Isaiah 40:11.) One can see the caring, tenderness and the love depicted there. I recall the work book I am doing. We are to look at what we have learned about love as we were raised. I have been praying and I am right now.

> 'Dear God please heal my heart that I may trust and love again, that I may open up to your love, your grace and your blessings, that I may open up to life itself. May I be cleansed and healed and come to feel your great love for your children. May I intimately know and feel that love. May it give me peace and strength and security. May I then in turn, be an even stronger beacon of Light for my children and grandson and others. Dear God in Heaven please hear this prayer. Please lay your healing hands upon my heart that I may know you even more.
>
> In Jesus name I pray.
> Amen.'

8

The first night of the retreat, our speaker Donna uses items as symbols for certain stages of her life. She asks us to think of what symbol comes to our mind for this stage of our own lives.

At first nothing comes up for me. Then I recall how the butterfly has been a symbol for me lately. Right now my life is about new beginnings, new growth, and new expansion. This week I sense how I am about to come into a period where I will be happier than I have ever been. I am realizing this because on inner levels I am finding more peace and love. I praise God for that!

We also talk about how prayer changes things. This is so important to remember. It is a reminder to me to continue to pray for my children, to assist them on their journeys.

'Pamela, trust the evolution of your own life. It will unfold perfectly, with the Lord's good help and Divine intervention.' These are the words I hear in my mind when I begin to think about when I get back home after the retreat.

In the last night's session, the leader asks us to match up and share and release whatever it is that is buried and needs to come out. I ask a dear friend if she will be willing to listen. We go for a walk. Over the week, I have been thinking of an incident that happened about thirty years prior. Just writing that number down helps me realize just how long ago that was and how much I have changed. I have become more aware of who I am. When I think of that time, I think of myself as a shell of a person, not really there, not conscious. For some reason, this incident comes into my thoughts. It is one I am ashamed of, aghast really that I would even think of doing such a thing.

So my dear friend and I go for our walk and I tell her. I cry. She prays. I realize that on a deep level, I feel unworthy of God's love. I see that on the inside I feel, 'Oh, what an absolutely horrible person I am.'

Jesus said to the adulterous, 'Go and sin no more' (KJV John 8:11.) He did not judge nor condemn her. He had dispersed the crowd who were ready to stone her by saying, 'He that is without sin among you, let him first cast a stone at her' (KJV John 8:7.)

I am here and now, ready, willing and able to

forgive myself. I am here and now, ready, willing and able to release the past. I am here and now, ready, willing and able to open my heart and to accept God's healing hands upon my heart.

Yes, dear Father hear this prayer. I am willing and open to your healing presence, to your healing gifts.

Thank You Father. Thank You.

9

As I am leaving the retreat, a lady approaches me. I am teary and emotional. She explains to me that before a butterfly can fly, there is a painful period they must go through before their wings can take flight. Having continued to relate to the butterfly symbol, I am grateful for her words.

Before there can be any real movement in one's life, one must come forth and reveal any indiscretions, hidden secrets, buried pain and/or unexpressed anguish.

Another big step for me is letting my family know that I have handled our dad's affairs inappropriately. This has to come out of the closet. I have to own up to what I have done and bear their possible wrath.

Knowing I am not alone, I inform them. Perfect timing for by the end of this same week, I am off to another spiritual retreat. With God in my heart, I am able to handle the various responses from family.

Thank you Father for giving me the courage to grow and for walking beside me through all the necessary steps.

Thank you Father for loving me unconditionally. Amen.

10

'I am come a light into the world that whosoever believeth on me shall not abide in darkness' (KJV John 12:46.)

I am at a Christian retreat. A new friend invited me. I am uncertain what this weekend entails yet am open to new experiences. Upon request I write a letter to Jesus.

Dear Jesus,

I sit here as you know at a weekend dedicated to you, to getting to know you better. It is a weekend for us to allow you to love us, to let that love in.

I stand in awe at the Divine timing of this retreat. It is right when I am dealing with so much guilt and shame, a burden I have been carrying.

The banner in one of the rooms says 'Expect a Miracle.'

This first night I feel your love around me. In my heart, I hear you invite me to come kneel before you and lay this burden of guilt at your feet. I feel you explain to me that I need not carry it anymore. Just as you broke the chains that bound me, I feel you now lift this burden from me. You show me that it is not others punishing me. It is me punishing myself. It is about me not having forgiven myself. It is me not fully accepting your gift of the cross, of your death for our sins. I must allow this gift into my very being.

At the retreat, I finally bury this burden, open my heart wide and lift my hands up to the sky. I proclaim within, 'Yes Father I open my heart to receive your gift, your love, your forgiveness.'

Thank you Father for assisting me along this 'Journey of Light.' Thank you so much.

11

Today I am going to a Butterfly House. Butterflies continue to fascinate me. They are such a spiritual symbol. I am watching one today as it drops out of its cocoon. It is all crunched up. Very gradually, the wings expand. I recall that as the blood is pumped through its veins, the wings unfold. Then, the butterfly stays very still to allow the wings to harden. All this is a process and must be done, before they can take flight.

Such a fascinating analogy, for indeed our own metamorphosis is similar. As God makes us anew, we, too, undergo a process which takes time. We feel completely changed from what we were, no longer a caterpillar. Yet even as we reach this point of coming out of our cocoon, there is still more process again before we can use our new wings.

I realize today that I have not given a lot of people a chance. I shut people out even before they can really get in. I judge and asses any possible relationship far too quickly and mostly out of fear. I pray this will change as I come out of my own cocoon. I pray for God to continue to heal my heart that gradually I will be more open to life and to love.

Dear Father please hear this prayer.
Amen

12

I had a big week at school. I am feeling very pressured and overwhelmed. My practicum is coming up soon. I do not feel ready. I still feel like this is not even the type of career I want. I am thinking, 'Pam, how does it feel? Give me an analogy.' I feel like I have been thrown in the deep end of a pool. I cannot swim. I am panicking. On the side of the pool is Sharon, our medical teacher, speaking to us, telling us what to do. I am crying. I feel this big weight on my shoulders. I pray to God about it. 'What am I to do?' I am starting to feel so afraid and anxious. So I think, 'See Jesus behind Sharon. Focus on Him.' This feels so much better. I stop panicking in the pool. I continue with this inner dialogue, 'Focus on your recent image of being out in the ocean of life (versus tied to the dock in a boat.) Your arms are outstretched welcoming life, trusting life, open to miracles and having faith.' I get in touch with this image. I start to feel better. I notice myself starting to breathe deeper and begin to relax. I continue within to be willing to trust and be calm. I feel in my heart God reminding me that if I do the school work, He will take care of the rest. So I think to myself this is what I have got to do. I have got to do my part and trust God with the other details.

It is now Sunday. I am at church. I have not been for several weeks. The sermon is in total harmony with what I have been going through. The Pastor is speaking about going through a crisis (the many sorts we have in our life.) We are to ask ourselves, 'Who is in control? Is it us, with our fears and anxieties, trying to control the outcome, while worrying and fretting, being afraid and anxious. Or are we able instead to be at peace, knowing God is in control.'

So, instead, the Pastor continues, we are to do our part and surrender and trust through prayer and give God the rest. We are to follow His guidance when and as it is given. By doing this, we can have peace through the crisis.

I write notes throughout the sermon. I am crying as I drive to meet up with a friend, tears of gratitude, and tears of awe and wonder. I think, 'I am on the right track in how I am going through this crisis in my life.'

I enjoy a wonderful afternoon with a dear friend I have not seen in a while. As I drive home later, I thank God. I feel like He wrapped me in love all day long. I feel so blessed and so grateful. As I pull into my driveway later, I feel so uplifted and refreshed.

The next time you are going through a challenging time, stop and remind yourself there is a God, you are His child (KJV Galatians 3:26) He loves you (KJV Isaiah 41:10.) If you have not already done so, open up your heart and let Him in. He is knocking at your door (KJV Revelation 3:20) waiting for you to open it.

Thank you Father for this amazing day!

13

Last night I had a dream with a beautiful message. In the dream, I open the fridge and in it is one of my old soup bowls. I recognize the design pattern on it. It is on the shelf at eye level. Inside the bowl is one wafer left, a wafer like Roman Catholics use in communion. It represents the body of Christ; in our church we use cubes of bread. As I stand here, with the fridge open, looking at the wafer, I hear a voice say, 'Let me be your sustenance.'

I awake and think, 'What a beautiful message!' It seems to confirm Sunday's sermon, 'Who is in control? Let God be.'

I feel so touched and honored to have received such a message.

Thank you God! Thank you.

14

My life experience has shown me that all prayer is answered. Sometimes I notice a billboard or the words on the side of a truck or the verse of a song. After a prayer I pay attention to what is going on around me. This morning I prayed about two things specifically. By the end of church both were answered within the dialogue of the sermon.

Having a personal relationship with God brings so many treasures. I learn to hear and trust this inner voice, not my voice, but His voice. This voice guides me on my life path, comforts me, protects me and answers my prayers.

It says in the Bible, 'Behold, I make all things new' (KJV, Rev 21:5.) This is so true, as my life shows. There is so much to learn, understand, absorb and then live by. I continue to be passionately hungry for it. I want to learn how to live a happy, prosperous, miraculous life. I believe we do not have to learn life lessons through pain or suffering. We can learn these same lessons through peace and love. I want to learn to live my life every day in an awareness of God's love, by living my life from my heart. I can allow my day to unfold in complete Divine harmony. I then know and trust that I will be in the right place at the right time doing exactly the right thing for the highest good of all. We can learn to allow life, every day, to meet all of our needs in miraculous and joyous ways.

I continue to learn and practice truths such as; 'For as a man thinketh in his heart, so is he' (KJV Proverbs 23: 7.) Jesus wants us to understand these important principles.

It has been said in so many ways over the years, recently by Rhonda Byrne in her books <u>The Secret</u> (Byrne, 2007) and <u>The Power</u> (Byrne, 2010.) One can use these insights to transform his or her life. We have the ability to change it from one of fear, drudgery, poverty and suffering to a higher level one of joy, comfort, peace, love, happiness and gratitude.

I give thanks for all I am learning. I open up my arms wide, outstretched, I say 'Yes,' to life's blessings. I do deserve to be happy. I do deserve the gifts, joy and love that God wants to bestow on me.

Thank you God. Thank you!

15

I am having a dream. I see a book cover. Is it my book? The title is <u>My Life is Always Great.</u> The accompanying picture is of a lady with a summer hat on, walking in a meadow picking flowers, to put in the basket she carries on her arm. You can sense she is at peace within herself and with her world. She eludes happiness and joy as she embraces God's amazing creations of beauty. She is loving life! I awaken. I realize I am now that woman.

As I go through another transition I am packing, I am not sure where I will be living or what career I will pursue. I keep my eyes focused on God. I pray for His will to be done for then my choices right now will be for the highest good of all.

I believe we really are very powerful within; we can be and do anything we choose. By these choices, we affect all the people around us, our family, our friends, the stranger in the grocery store, our fellow employees, the person in the car coming towards us, everyone.

My daughter paid me a compliment a few days ago. She said, "Mom you know how you say that the best thing you can do for your family is to continue to grow, learn and be the best you can be?'

"Yes," I answer.

"Well, I am grateful Mom for what you are doing. This means I will always have a healthy parent."

This inner walk is my passion. I have had counselling: taken self-help courses, read books, done hypnotherapy. I have my Masters in Reiki: received energy healing, explored various churches, listened to guided meditation tapes, journaled, fasted, gone to spiritual retreats. I moved from A to B many times. I have gone back to school in my late fifties: stretched myself, come to know God, surrendered my life to Him, been reborn, restored and forgiven. I have forgiven myself and others. As I continue to get it right, then my ripple becomes stronger, more positive. For this, I am grateful.

Thank you Father.

16

While praying to God for guidance during this transition period, I am given an analogy. Just as the Red Sea parted and people were led away from danger, so too the path is being made for me (KJV Exodus 14:21.) God is preparing the way, going before me. I only have to follow Him. I am safe, guided and protected.

Thank you so much Father for all your guidance, right down to specific steps. I am so grateful. You know in my heart that I want only what is for the highest good of all.

17

I just had a visit with my elderly father. He lives in a Long Term Care Center. He has dementia. I am frustrated at the inability to communicate with my dad. I decide to lay down when I get home.

I am in the middle of a dream. I am reaching out to my dad, standing with my arms outstretched. I look down at my feet. They are at the edge of a line. I am unable to cross the line. My feet are sticking to this tar substance. I am stretching out my arms, wanting with every ounce of my being to reach out and connect with my dad.

Dad is in his wheelchair a fair distance from me on the other side of this huge room. He is turned away from me though I can still see his eyes. They are closed. He appears to be sleeping. He opens his eyes and gazes out the window. I sense he is not really focusing on anything. He has this faraway look in his eyes.

Now Jesus appears. He sees my dilemma. He stretches out His arms as far as He can, one towards dad, the other towards me. Jesus spreads His legs for a stronger stance, still stretching out His arms as far as He can. He is covering the great distance between dad and I.

I awake. I realize that through Jesus, dad and I do stay connected. I no longer feel frustrated and upset.

Thank you Father for the comfort this dream brings to me.

Thank you for the understanding that through the love in our hearts, dad and I are always connected.

18

This is my first time creating a folder on my new laptop. I want to save some quotes from the church service I attended this morning.

"….a journey out of brokenness."

"There is no heart that God cannot heal. No life that He cannot change. None!"

I am thinking about how far the healing of my heart has progressed. Two years ago I was seeing a counsellor; he was assisting me with the journey of healing my heart after leaving a third unhealthy relationship. At that time, I could not even look at a man. I would drop my head as I walked by, even something as simple as passing a man coming out of the library.

Now I make eye contact, have conversations and even entertain the idea of dating again.

Thank you Father for this healing process.

19

I recall writing as a teenager, 'Love is the answer. Forgiveness is the key.'

I am sitting in church listening to a sermon about self-forgiveness and forgiveness of others. The pastor is explaining that in God's eyes, once we truly repent, all is forgiven and it is done. That's it. We do not need to carry that remorse forever with us. 'What sin?' the pastor says, to illustrate his point. It feels like these words are speaking directly to me. I am to let go, move on, and stop punishing myself.

Have you ever stood back and seen that you have unconsciously set up the circumstances in your life, like unhealthy relationships, in order to punish yourself? I have.

> 'Thy word is a lamp unto my feet and a light unto my path' (KJV Psalm 119:105.)

Thank you Father for your words today, speaking straight to my heart, shedding light on my understanding.

Amen.

20

It is my mother's funeral today. As I am being driven to the church, I speak to her in my mind. 'Mom, if you want me to do this you are going to have to help me.' I am to say her eulogy.

As I sit in the pew waiting my turn, I am taking notice of what the minister is doing, speaking clearly, loudly and slowly. This way her message is being heard. I make a mental note to do the same.

I love my mom. I miss her. I recall feeling earlier this morning, 'I do not know if I can do this.' This meaning live and function through the day of my mother's funeral. It is all rather surreal, losing a parent, planning the funeral, saying their eulogy.

It is my turn to speak.

'As I was dressing today I found myself choosing the things that reminded me of my mother, like the pearls she gave me on my wedding day and this dress I never got to wear for our next luncheon date....'

As I continue, I make eye contact with the crowd. I am saying all the things I feel mom wants me to say, that she loves these people, that she is grateful to each and every one of them for filling her life with love and joy.

I next share a dream I had. I am pushing my mom in a wheelchair. I look up. Jesus is walking towards me. He explains to me that He will now take my mother the rest of the way home.

Throughout the funeral, I feel her close to me, in my heart, giving me encouragement and love.

As the day draws to an end, my spiritual beliefs give me comfort.

Thank you Father for the promise of eternal life. (KJV 1 John 5:13)

21

I decide to go for a labyrinth walk at church. I am tired after work and am thinking of not going. However, I feel God nudging me to go. I am feeling more confident now in this decision. I know that once again, as before, a labyrinth walk will be an incredible experience, truly a blessing.

I gaze at the tea light candles circling the labyrinth. I decide to shed things on the way in to the core of the labyrinth and to take on things on the way back out. I want to shed all judgmental thoughts of people, to let go of all that type of thinking. I choose instead to just notice and observe. I just look, see and carry on, with no emotional judgement. I apply this to myself as well as others. This gives me more freedom. I accept others for who they are as individuals and also for where they are on their own path.

During my labyrinth walk, I am at times

watching my feet. 'What footprints am I leaving behind as I walk this journey of life?' I ponder.

It feels as if God is brushing away dirt and sand covering my heart. I hear His voice within my heart asking me if I want more than just my little apartment experience. I hear Him encouraging me to open my heart, to open myself up to all the gifts, blessings and prosperities that He wants to give me. This inner voice explains to me that life is meant to be full, rich, abundant and joyful.

I feel myself opening up as I hear my inner reply back that yes I do choose the full, rich life that God wants for me. (KJV John 10:10)

As I walk the labyrinth, I affirm within: I now choose to open myself up fully to all the prosperity, abundance and fullness of life, to the life that God wants for me, has intended for me. I then visualize myself with arms stretched out open wide to the sky above me. I am ready to receive.

Thank you Father once again for the gifts you have bestowed on me on this blessed day.

Amen.

22

As I sit down to dinner, I look out at the evening sky. The position and shape of the clouds creates a picture of the Earth as it would appear from a distance. I think about the magnetic energy force that holds our planet in place. I recall books I have read about energy and the Law of Attraction such as Rhonda Byrne's <u>The Secret</u> (Byrne, 2006) and Ester Hick's books of Abraham (Hicks, 1981.) These authors talk about things being drawn to us like a magnet. Our thoughts send out frequencies into the universe attracting back to us like a magnet whatever it is we are focusing on.

'And all things whatsoever ye shall ask in prayer, believing ye shall receive' (KJV Matthew 21:22.) I think of this verse as I recall how my new car showed up in my life, at the right time and for the amount I wanted to spend.

We are able to become more powerful in our

life, attracting to us only more joy, more good by changing our thoughts.

> '...whatsoever things are honest, whatsoever things are just, whatsoever thing are pure, whatsoever things are of good report...think on these things' (KJV Philippians 4:8.)

I recently listened to an audio book entitled <u>Making Your Thoughts Work for You</u> by Wayne Dyer and Byron Katie.

Thank you Father for this beautiful day and this insightful wisdom.

23

I am in a deep trance like state. I have the following experience.

I hear within a voice calling out to me, asking for me to follow. A hand is extended, encouraging me. It feels right and safe to continue. Tears flow down my face. I experience all this sadness and hurt I am carrying being taken from me. It is time to let it go and to wave good-bye to all of it. I am being encouraged to bid it all farewell versus staying stuck within this immense sadness, hurt and pain. I am told to turn my head and my body and look forward. I turn and wave good-bye to all the painful emotions and look forward.

Then I see a vision of Jesus in my mind. I see Him in the same likeness as a picture I had seen earlier today. He looks so real, in human form, in this portrait. I stopped in the store and stared at it for a while.

As my dream like experience continues, I join

Jesus on a gravel path, leading up a steep hill. Then a vision of Mother Mary appears also. She is now on the other side of me as we walk along.

When we arrive at the top of the hill, they show me a city in the valley below. The city is all aglow. Full of compassion, Jesus speaks to me in my dream.

As I write this now, I do not recall His exact words. The awareness of being loved, forever, always and unconditionally, this is what is forever embedded in my heart.

This is a very intense experience. To this day, I can close my eyes and still feel both Jesus and Mother Mary beside me in that dream.

Thank you Father for this amazing experience!

24

I am in a Dollar Store line up. As I approach the cashier, I ask her, "How are you?"

"I am living a dream," she answers.

'Wow!' I think to myself.

I am somewhat taken aback by this unconventional response.

As she does my financial transaction and bags my items, I observe this young girl with interest. I decide to ask her outright, "What made you respond that way?"

She pauses and looks at me. I gaze back, noticing her various piercings as I do so. She definitely has a unique presentation.

"Well," she begins, "I love my job and the fact that I do not have to get up early for school tomorrow. Also, it is a busy day today so the time is flying by."

I reply, "What a great attitude. Yes, there is always something for which we can be grateful."

As I drive home, I continue to ponder our exchange and especially her choice of words: 'I am living a dream.'

I think about my own life and how I also am 'living a dream.' With prosperity in every area of my life, a healthy body, a job I love and with great coworkers. My family are all well and healthy and most live close by, I have a great apartment and on and on. My life is full of blessings.

As I park the car by my apartment building, I think about the side walk chalk note I had come across and written about in my first book. What a difference this girl's comment was from that negative one. Hers is full of life and joy. 'I am living a dream.' The other was full of anger and despair. 'Don't grow up. It's a trap.'

As I walk up to my third floor apartment, I think with that kind of attitude and knowing the power of our thoughts this young girl will indeed continue to live a life of a positive happy dream.

Thank you Father for our paths crossing on this blessed day!

25

Recording my personal 'Journey of Light' is a message also that life is not about money, career or material things. It is about the little ones at our feet. It is about asking ourselves, 'What are those around us learning from the way we are living our lives? What example are we setting?'

Recently, I was getting out some old photos to look at with my now adult children. I came across a school assignment. For a Grade 9 religion project, my daughter was asked to pull out photos of her mother and record underneath what she had learned from her. She received a top score with an 'Excellent' comment written beside it.

Here is what my daughter wrote:

'She taught me to be positive and happy even when times get rough.'

'My mom has always been an inspiration especially when it comes to opening up and appreciating others just the way they are.'

'She always said not to listen to what people said but what was more important was how you see yourself.'

'My mom believed that if someone is in your life (like a friend) they are there to teach you or help you get through a rough time. Once you lose touch with them or they decide not to be a part of your life, it was their time to leave you.'

'My mom has taught me that no matter how small or full your heart is there is always room to love another person.'

'She has taught me to be thankful for what we have because she said we are very lucky and blessed with all the things we have.'

'My mom probably doesn't know it but she has taught me to slow down and make the most of each and every day.'

'My mom has showed me that I should not judge people before I know them, because they really are great.'

'My mother has said that everyone has a voice within to help them when they are in trouble or in doubt. Now I can sometimes hear that voice when I really need it.'

'My mother has always appreciated her health and that has had such an impact on me. I now thank God for how lucky I am to be so healthy and to recognize it once and a while.'

'My mom has taught me to be more honest and to speak up to other people and not let them walk all over you.'

'When it comes to patience my mom has taught me many things. I can be so on edge sometimes and she showed me that not everything is wrong and just to breathe.'

Thank you Father for the honour and privilege of being a parent.

26

One of life's special moments is when your grandson runs along the sidewalk to greet you, yelling with arms outstretched wide, "Grandma. Grandma." This little one is now soon to be nine. How quickly the years go by!

I am having this same grandson for a sleepover tonight. At this particular place of residence, we have only had a few of these all niters. Needless to say, it is a real treat for all!

This morning my grandson has an upset and his day has not begun well at all. My daughter calls and tells me about it. I am more determined than ever to make our time together extra special. I am soon off to the store for a bag of apples.

You see my grandson loves making apple pie with grandma. He enjoys feasting off the apple skins as I peel the apples. Then he continues on with the munching of the apple cores themselves after the apples are chopped up. Of course, grandma leaves some apple around the core for him to enjoy. He helps with the pastry roll out. Sprinkling on the cinnamon and poking the top crust with a fork are his final touches before the pie goes in the oven.

Today I am having sticky difficulty with a new pastry recipe. He is restless. I give him my white-board and marker to play with in the interim. Later when I look at the board, my grandson has printed, 'Jesus Loves You and Me.' beside this he has drawn a red heart and a happy face. Off to the side, he prints, 'Grandma and Aidan.' This time he draws a boy with a big smile and writes, 'Love,' beside him. I knew his mom had been working with him on identifying feelings. I am so joyful when I see what he has done. This is his way of telling me he is feeling so much better than he had at the beginning of his day. He feels loved and happy now. That is what any grandma wants to know.

Later, after supper I am getting our dessert, pie and ice-cream. I do not usually have ice-cream in the house. My grandson asks about what kind I got. I say to look in the freezer and see. "Cookies and Cream, my favorite!' he exclaims. "Mine too," I say. I cut the pie and dish out the ice-cream. I ask him, "How is that?" and as he leaves the kitchen, dessert plate in hand, he replies, "I have everything I need." 'Wow,' I think. 'Now that's what I like to hear!'

The next night is my granddaughter Emma's turn for a sleepover. She is so very excited. She wakes up early in the morning and puts on her prettiest dress. Mom has to explain to her that her turn is not for several hours yet. "I understand Mommy," she replies in her mature four year old voice.

Once she arrives, we immediately set about to make a batch of chocolate chip cookies. She also loves helping Grandma in the kitchen. "Can I do the eggs Grandma? Can I do the eggs?" This child loves cracking them open on the side of the bowl. She is such a good mixer too! She twirls that batter with all the strength her young muscles can muster. I take a great picture of her in the kitchen with her pretty dress and full wide brimmed hat, holding the bowl while she stirs away with her other hand. What a beautiful sight!

At supper time, as I am about to say grace, my granddaughter speaks up, "I will say it Grandma." This is her first time. It touches my heart. The following day for breakfast and for lunch, she asks again to say grace. I am so proud of her. I also realize that the example I set, is indeed noticed by the little ones.

As we watch a film, she squeezes in beside me on the arm chair. She wraps her arm around mine and strokes my hand. "Love and happy," she says. I remember again that my daughter has been working with the children on identifying their feelings. How honoured I am to hear the positive ones that my granddaughter is feeling as she sits beside her grandma.

Thank you Heavenly Father for the gift of grandchildren. May I always be all that they need me to be. May you guide me on what that is, and how to fulfill it. May they always feel safe and loved. May my life reflect your shining Light within it for them to see.

Amen.

27

My grandson is over for supper and a visit. Spontaneously, I reach over and touch his arm. I say aloud "I love you very much Aidan." He responds immediately. "I know you do."

Wow! That is like an arrow right to my heart – in a good way. I feel warm and tingly inside.

Thinking about it more later, I realize that response means more to me than when he replies "I love you too Grandma." For when he says, "I know you do," this tells me that he feels loved by me. This, of course, is always my intention. His reply is the best gift any grandmother could ever ask to receive. My grandson's comment reflects back to me his experience and that my actions towards him are perceived as loving and respectful. He sees my behavior matching my words. This relationship is indeed healthy, strong and secure.

One of my prayers for humanity has been that people everywhere would know that they are loved and that they are never alone. I mean this in a spiritual sense.

I have also been praying specifically that my grandchildren would know that they are loved, especially since the recent separation of their parents, even more the reason for my excitement at his response.

Thank you Father for this day and for the joy those four words brought to my heart. Thank you!

28

I love it when I wake up and discover I have slept through the night, no frequent pee breaks, no leg cramps, and no painful body parts. When I awaken on such glorious mornings, I already know it is going to be an awesome day.

I reach for my headset and immediately decide to complement the day even further by listening to a guided meditation.

I close my eyes and pray to Jesus that I may feel His Presence envelope me. As the meditation draws to close, I ask and affirm that throughout this day, I will be in the right place at the right time doing precisely that right thing for the Highest good of all. I ask that I will make all the right choices in both my personal and professional life. I ask that I may be a strong beacon of Light both for myself and others. I ask that I will be guided from within on all things.

I get out of bed knowing that as I open up and say 'Yes' to life, life says 'Yes' back to me. I understand clearly that it is all up to me, that I create the tone of my life. I decide. It is my responsibility. No one else can make my life the way I want it to be. Only I can do that. I do this by choosing my thoughts carefully. I choose positive grateful thoughts, self-affirming thoughts. 'For as he thinketh in his heart so is he' (KJV Proverbs 23:7.)

I practice being my own best friend. When negative things come up, I do not feed the beast as I call it. Rather, I focus on what I want, not on what I do not want. I apply self-discipline in all areas of my life. This keeps me from falling down any more black holes. I have been there. I have learned what I need to do so I do not go back there.

Thank you Father for this 'Journey of Light.' All parts of it have led me to where I am now, for this I am eternally grateful.

Amen.

29

How fitting that the conclusion of this book is aligned with further expansion and growth of my own 'Journey of Light.' This journey is an ongoing process, evolution if you will. I am so excited, filled with anticipation as I enter yet another phase of this spiritual journey.

I have several ornaments and wall hangings in my apartment. 'You are a Miracle. Expect Miracles. Believe in your Self.' I have a poster in my office, 'Believe in Miracles. For with God all things are possible' (KJV Matthew 19:26.)

Spending time in meditation, going within, using the tools that I am given whether it is books, CDs, DVDs, people, places and things, all aspects of this journey is Divinely taken care of with utmost certainty. I have only to desire it with every ounce of my being. Then allow it to happen, to unfold, so naturally, so perfectly.

I invite you to embark on your own unique

'Journey of Light.' Begin the journey that will change your life forever more. What will happen is like a flower opening into a full, glorious bloom, you too will open up, becoming more and more of who you are, who you truly are meant to be.

For this blessing shall you also say -
Thank you Father! Thank you!

30

Let your Light shine bright within your heart.

Let your words always speak the truth.

Let your actions match what you proclaim.

May you look out at the world with eyes of compassion.

May you touch the hearts of many with your subtle grace.

Let God lead your way.

Listen to the inner voice inside your heart.

It will show you the way.

In all things, be grateful.

Let this be your continual prayer.

Teach others what you know.

Be a guide for them.

Be a beacon of Light.

Take the first initial steps.

God will do the rest.

31

I made a promise to myself last night that I would go the church today where I was baptized six years ago on Easter Sunday. I want to honour the anniversary of that special day.

I have not been to a service at this church since the pastor I knew left for a new placement. As I take a seat, I look around me. I see some familiar faces. I observe the band setting up on the stage. There are some changes in the musicians and the singers. I am looking forward to hearing the new pastor speak.

Within the sermon, I hear a reminder that the church is human. I, who indeed had been sitting here judging some changes, am now moved to be more compassionate and accepting.

The pastor speaks about the disciple Peter when he denies knowing Jesus (KJV Matthew 26:34.) At the conclusion of the service he again returns to the story of Peter. We are to draw an analogy to ourselves who also may have had much to be forgiven.

Now as we proclaim our love for Jesus, it is our mission, like Peter's (KJV John 21:17) to go out and spread the word of Jesus.

I can feel tears fill my eyes as these words go right to my heart.

I am thinking of my own 'Journey of Light' and the publication of this book.

Thank you Father for knowing my needs, giving to me through today's sermon, the encouragement I needed to proceed.

Amen.

32

It is now a week later. I find myself driving into the city to attend a different church this time. This one also I have not been to for quite some time. It is a much longer distance from my home. In the past I have enjoyed it immensely.

Once again, I look around and see subtle changes, like the musicians and singers, the same pastor though.

As I sit here, I reflect on the distance I have travelled on my 'Journey of Light.' I have passed through bankruptcy, drug use, cigarette addiction, one night stands, daily use of alcohol, unhealthy relationships, theft and lies. I have broken most of the commandments (KJV Exodus 20). I think about last week's sermon about Peter.

I am in the middle of editing this book. Today, the pastor has us do an exercise. My interpretation leads me to close my eyes and lay my concerns at God's feet. Within my heart, I hear a reply that reminds me that 'the book is not about me.' I am to focus on the book's true purpose, sharing what He can do in our lives, that readers may be inspired to invite Him in to their own life. I am to set aside my tiredness and my editing concerns.

Once again, I am in awe as God continues to have me be in the right place at the right time to receive the message He has for me.

Thank you Father for walking along side of me each day.

Thank you Father most of all for your amazing grace. (KJV Ephesians 2: 8-9)

33

Like at my baptism, I shed tears now of humility, joy and wonder. I am concluding this book by listening to the well- known song 'Amazing Grace' (John Newton 1779.) I stand back and look at this book project in awe. All aspects of it have unfolded so Divinely perfect, same as His love. I am continuously reminded to never doubt His daily presence in my life.

I pray now that by sharing my 'Journey of Light' that you also have this same awareness of God in your life. If you cannot find Him there, then I pray for you to invite Him in, right here, right now. He is here waiting for you to open up your heart to Him. '…thou shalt weep no more: he will be very gracious unto thee at the voice of thy cry…he will answer thee' (KJV Isaiah 30:19.) God lives within each of us. I invite you to remove your wall of doubt and fear. You will find Him then. He is there, waiting for you to choose.

Thank you Father for all the stages this 'Journey of Light' encompasses. Thank you for walking with me every step along the way.

Amen.

REFERENCES

Byrne, R. (2006) *The Secret*; (2010) *The Power*

Dyer, W. and Katie, B. (2007) *Making Your Thoughts Work For You*

Hicks, E. (1981) *The Law of Attraction: The Basic Teachings Of Abraham*

King James Version, The Bible

Lucado, M. (2009) *Fearless*

Printed in the United States
By Bookmasters